Contents

Some words are shown in bold, **like this**.
You can find out what they mean by looking in the glossary.

What is gravity?

▲ **This astronaut's hair is floating above her head as she tries to brush it in a space shuttle where there is very little gravity.**

You enter a room full of people. They are all standing in midair. One man waves at you in a friendly way. He turns a few somersaults as he glides over to shake your hand.

What is unusual about this scene? There is no **gravity**. On Earth, people don't stand in midair. Gravity keeps them firmly on the ground.

That is how most people think of gravity. It is the force that pulls us down. If you could magically switch off gravity, most things on Earth would float into space.

THE STORY BEHIND

GRAVITY

Sean Stewart Price

7000037011220

www.raintreepublishers.co.uk
Visit our website to find out more information about Raintree books.

To order:
Phone 0845 6044371
Fax +44 (0) 1865 312263
Email myorders@capstonepub.co.uk

Customers from outside the UK please telephone +44 1865 312262

Raintree is an imprint of Capstone Global Library Limited, a company incorporated in England and Wales having its registered office at 7 Pilgrim Street, London, EC4V 6LB – Registered company number: 6695582

"Raintree" is a registered trademark of Pearson Education Limited, under licence to Capstone Global Library Limited.

Text © Capstone Global Library Limited 2009
First published in hardback in 2009
Paperback edition first published in 2010
The moral rights of the proprietor have been asserted.

All rights reserved. No part of this publication may be reproduced in any form or by any means (including photocopying or storing it in any medium by electronic means and whether or not transiently or incidentally to some other use of this publication) without the written permission of the copyright owner, except in accordance with the provisions of the Copyright, Designs and Patents Act 1988 or under the terms of a licence issued by the Copyright Licensing Agency, Saffron House, 6–10 Kirby Street, London EC1N 8TS (www.cla.co.uk). Applications for the copyright owner's written permission should be addressed to the publisher.

Edited by Louise Galpine, Abby Colich, and Diyan Leake
Designed by Philippa Jenkins and Artistix
Original illustrations © Capstone Global Library Ltd
Illustrated by Gary Slater/Specs Art
Picture research by Mica Brancic
Originated by Modern Age Repro House Ltd
Printed and bound in China by CTPS

ISBN 978 0 431114 90 3 (hardback)
13 12 11 10 09
10 9 8 7 6 5 4 3 2 1

ISBN 978 0 431115 04 7 (paperback)
14 13 12 11 10
10 9 8 7 6 5 4 3 2 1

British Library Cataloguing in Publication Data
Price, Sean
The story behind gravity. – (True stories)
531.1'4
A full catalogue record for this book is available from the British Library.

Acknowledgements
We would like to thank the following for permission to reproduce photographs: AKG-images pp. **6** (© Erich Lessing), **12**; Art Archive p. **15**; Corbis pp. **5** (© moodboard), 10 (© Bettmann), 13 (Stocktrek), 14 (© Bettmann), **17** (© Owaki/Kulla), **20** (© Jim Sugar); Getty Images p. **27** (The Image Bank/© Kauko Helavuo); http://lifeboat.com/ex/space.habitats p. **22**; © NASA p. **11**; Photolibrary pp. **18** (© Image Source), **19** (© Image 100); Photolibrary.com p. **9** (Robert Harding Travel); Science Photo Library pp. **4** (© NASA), **16** (NASA), **23** (© NASA), **24** (© Joe Tucciarone), **25** (© European Space Agency), **26** (© Joe Tucciarone); Shutterstock pp. **iii** (© Horatiu Bota), **8** (© Jurgen Ziewe); The Bridgeman Art Library p. **7** (Louvre, Paris/© Giraudon).

Cover photograph of a rock falling through water reproduced with permission of Getty Images (Stone/Ryan McVay).

Every effort has been made to contact copyright holders of any material reproduced in this book. Any omissions will be rectified in subsequent printings if notice is given to the publisher.

All the Internet addresses (URLs) given in this book were valid at the time of going to press. However, due to the dynamic nature of the Internet, some addresses may have changed, or sites may have changed or ceased to exist since publication. While the author and publisher regret any inconvenience this may cause readers, no responsibility for any such changes can be accepted by either the author or the publisher.

But gravity is even bigger than that. Gravity is the attraction between any two objects. The more **mass** (size or bulk) an object has, the bigger its gravitational pull. That means gravity affects the whole **universe** (everything that exists). It keeps the moon spinning around Earth. It also keeps Earth turning around the sun. It keeps the sun and planets moving around the centre of our galaxy. A galaxy is a large group of stars and planets held together by gravity.

Gravity is a very weak force. For instance, it is not as strong as magnetism. A magnet can easily pull up another magnet, defeating gravity. But unlike magnetism and other natural forces, gravity's reach extends billions of miles. In fact, every object in the universe gives off a gravitational pull on every other object. But that pull is so slight that we usually don't feel it.

The mystery of gravity 

Scientists know all this about *how* gravity works. But they still don't know *why* gravity works. Why do larger objects attract things more than smaller objects? That remains one of science's greatest unexplained mysteries.

▼ Skydivers float down to Earth because of the force of gravity.

Newton's world

In 1666, the English scientist Isaac Newton had a flash of insight. According to legend, it happened one day when he saw an apple fall from a tree. Newton realised that some invisible force had pushed the apple to the ground. He also discovered that the same force kept the moon spinning around Earth. In fact, this force – **gravity** – held the whole **universe** together. Newton not only saw these things. He also came up with a mathematical explanation for how they worked. This helped people to accept that he was correct.

◀ This portrait of Isaac Newton was painted soon after he published his ideas about gravity.

384–322 BCE

Greek scientist Aristotle believes that Earth lies at the centre of the universe. He also thinks the sun and stars move around Earth on giant glass balls.

1000 BCE

0

Newton versus Aristotle

Before Newton, most people did not even know about gravity. Instead, many believed the ideas of a scientist from ancient Greece called Aristotle. In the 300s BCE, Aristotle declared that Earth was the centre of the universe. He said the sun and stars were part of giant glass balls. Those balls spun around Earth and never changed. Aristotle also said that part of the reasons that heavy stones fell was because they were attracted to the centre of the universe. Other scientists before Newton had challenged Aristotle's ideas. But Newton proved these ideas wrong for good.

Isaac Newton and the philosopher's stone

Newton was a great scientist. But much of his interest lay with alchemy. Alchemists often combined science with magic. Many of them – including Newton – tried to create the "philosopher's stone". This stone supposedly would give someone everlasting life. Of course, Newton was wrong. Alchemy was not a science. But discoveries made by alchemists helped create the science of chemistry.

Aristotle lived from 384 to 322 BCE. This is a copy of a marble statue of him made during the 300s.

1666

English scientist Isaac Newton realises that the force that causes an apple to fall to the ground is the same one that causes the moon to go around Earth. He uses maths to explain how gravity and motion work.

1600 CE

▲ This picture shows how the planets in our solar system travel around the sun.

The sun and planets

To understand Newton's ideas, you must understand our **solar system**. Our solar system is made up of our sun and the planets that go around it. About 4.6 billion years ago, our solar system was a giant cloud of gas, dust, and ice. Gravity caused the cloud to shrink. The inner part became the sun. The outer pieces took shape as the planets.

The sun is a star. It is by far the biggest object in our solar system. About one million Earths would fit inside it. The sun has a much greater **mass** than any of the planets. This means that it also has the strongest gravity.

Into orbit

The sun's gravity keeps Earth and other planets from drifting off into space. Instead, they **orbit** (go around) the sun. But Earth does not travel in a perfect circle. Instead, its orbit is elliptical (oval-shaped).

Earth is one of the sun's **satellites**. A satellite is an object that goes around another object. The other planets are satellites, too. At the same time, the moon is a satellite of Earth. Earth is about six times bigger than the moon. So, Earth's gravity keeps the moon in orbit.

Moonstruck

There are a lot of legends about the moon. Many people believe that full moons cause crime to rise and dogs to bite more often. People are said to go a bit mad. In fact, the word *lunatic* means "moonstruck". There is no proof that the moon does any of these things. But the gravitational pull between Earth and the moon does create the ocean tides. The water levels in the ocean rise and fall every 12 and a half hours.

▼ **Gravity between the moon and Earth causes the tides that may carry seaweed on to a beach.**

Gravity, weight, and motion

An elephant weighs more than a person. A person weighs more than a squirrel. Those ideas are easy for people to understand. But most people do not understand why. An elephant is heavier because **gravity** pulls on it more. Gravity pulls more because the elephant has more **mass** than a person or a squirrel. Weight is simply what we call gravity's pull. The greater the mass an object has, the greater its weight.

◀ **The Italian scientist Galileo studied the effects of gravity. This sketch shows him at the Tower of Pisa. He is experimenting with the speed of falling objects.**

384–322 BCE
Greek scientist Aristotle believes that objects of different weights fall at different speeds.

1000 BCE | 500 BCE | 0

Aristotle versus Galileo

In the 300s **BCE**, Aristotle said that objects of different weights would fall at different speeds. But in the early 1600s **CE**, the Italian scientist Galileo Galilei proved Aristotle wrong. Galileo showed that objects fall at the same speed no matter what their weight. Drop two balls of different sizes and weights from the same height. They will both hit the ground at the same time.

Gravity causes all objects to accelerate (speed up) at an exact rate near Earth's surface. That rate is 9.8 metres (32 feet) per second **squared**. ("Squared" means a number multiplied by itself.) Why don't more massive objects fall faster? Isaac Newton found that **inertia** slows them down. Inertia is resistance to change in motion. Massive objects must overcome more resistance, or inertia, in order to move.

A space experiment

In 1971 *Apollo 15* astronauts conducted an experiment on the moon. Which would fall faster – a hammer or a feather? Both fell at the same speed. On Earth, the air around us creates air resistance. Air resistance would slow down the feather. But in space, there is no air. So, there is no air resistance. Only gravity is at work.

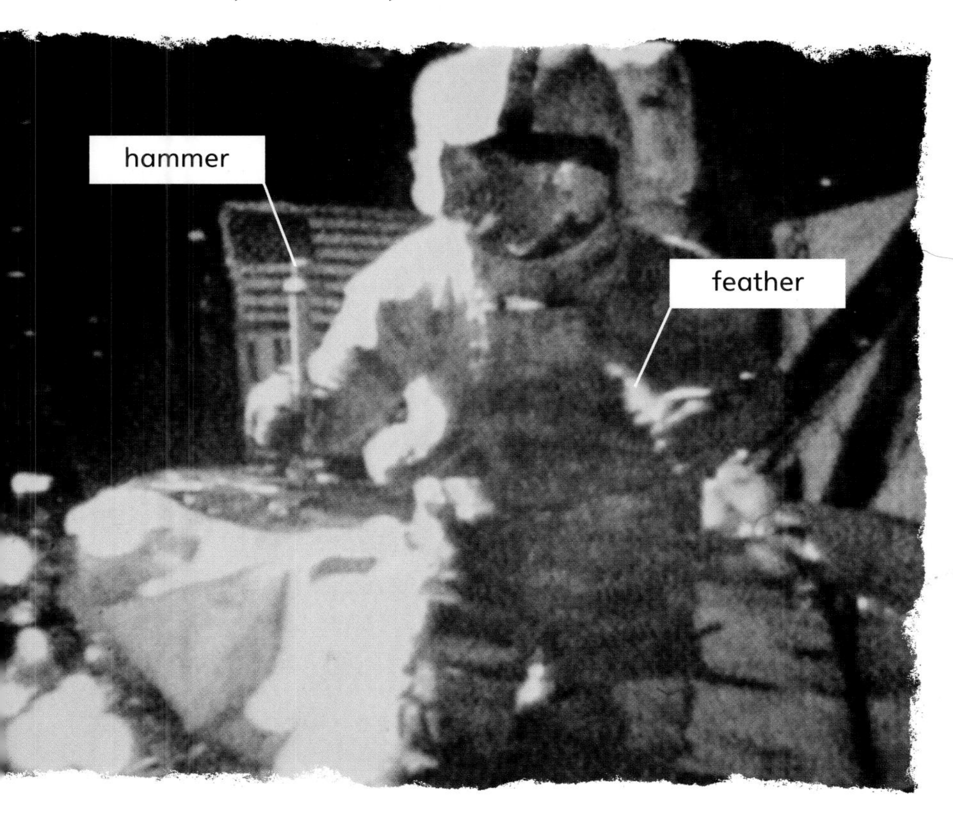

◀ **This photo shows the *Apollo 15* crew's experiment with the hammer and feather.**

early 1600s

Italian scientist Galileo Galilei does gravity experiments. They prove Aristotle wrong. Among other things, Galileo finds that objects of different weights fall at the same speed.

1660s

English scientist Isaac Newton explains the concept of inertia.

1600 CE

▶ Very few people understand Einstein's theories, but many people recognize his face. It has become the image that people use to illustrate the idea of someone who is very clever.

Albert Einstein

In the early 1900s, the German-born US scientist Albert Einstein further changed the way people view motion and gravity. Up until then, most people saw gravity the way Newton had explained it. But Einstein began explaining some things that Newton could not.

Few people expected such big things from Einstein. He was not a good student. One professor called him a lazy dog. But Einstein was clever. The ideas he came up with for gravity are called the General Theory of Relativity. Unfortunately, Einstein's theory is very complicated. Some have joked that only 12 people in the world understand it!

1905
German-born US scientist Albert Einstein comes up with his General Theory of Relativity.

1900 1910 1920

Einstein's mistake

In 1917 Einstein's maths showed that the **universe** was growing in size. But at the time, scientists believed that gravity kept the universe the same size. So, Einstein changed his maths slightly to agree with their belief. But later scientists showed that the universe really is expanding, despite gravity's pull. Einstein called changing his original ideas his biggest mistake.

Einstein and the atomic bomb

Even people who don't understand Einstein's theories have heard of his most famous equation. It is $E = mc^2$. In this formula, *E* stands for **energy** (a form of power), *m* stands for mass, and *c* stands for the speed of light, which is squared in this equation. With this equation, Einstein showed that mass and energy can be changed from one to the other. In 1945 scientists used this equation to turn mass into energy. They created the **atomic bomb**. It was the first bomb powerful enough to destroy an entire city.

This photo shows an atomic bomb being tested in the Nevada desert in the United States.

1945
The atomic bomb is created.

1930 1940 1950

Defying gravity

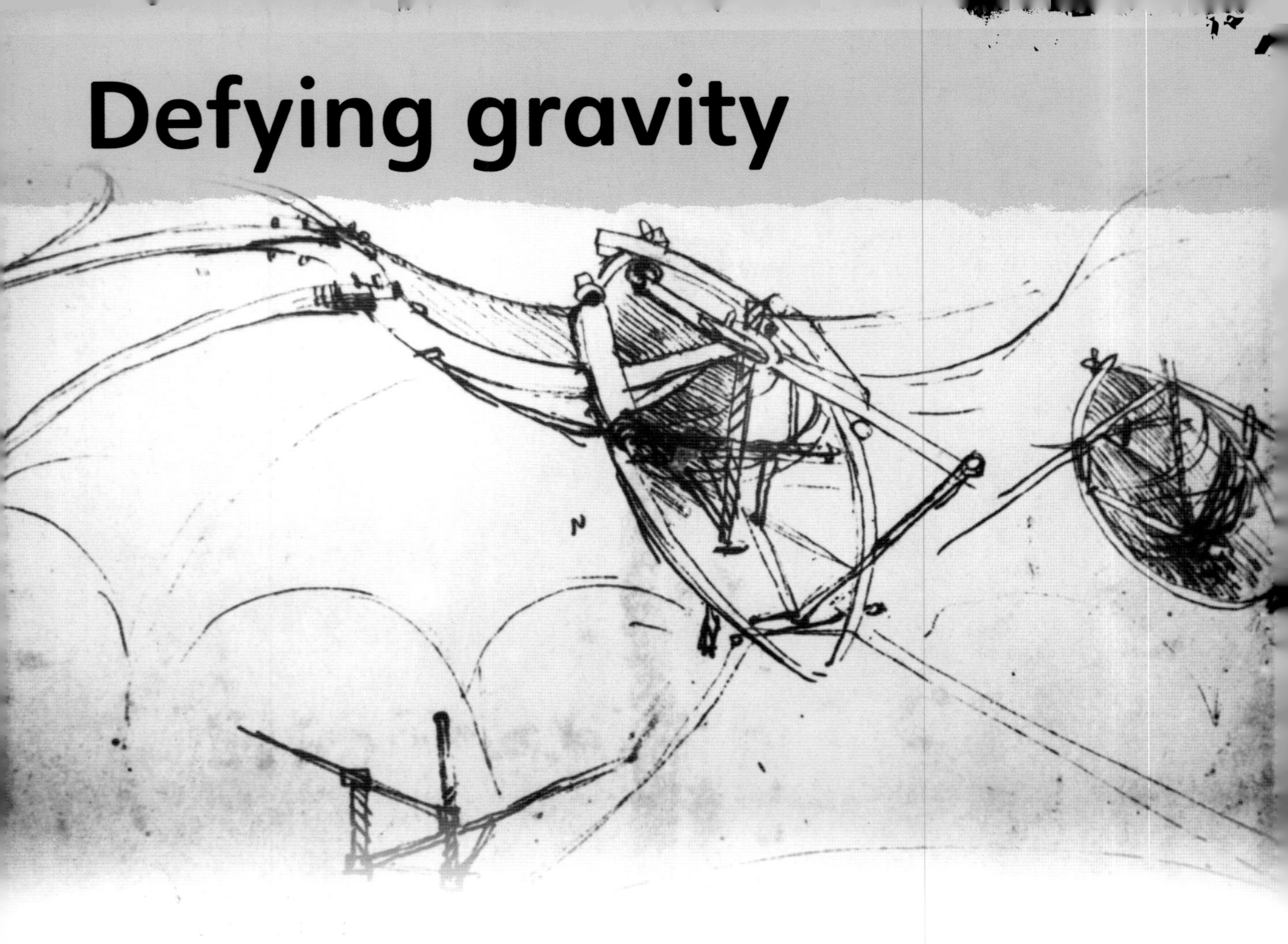

▲ **This drawing shows some of Leonardo da Vinci's designs for flying machines.**

For centuries, humans dreamed of flying. But it took a long time to overcome **gravity**.

1485–1500: Italian artist and inventor Leonardo da Vinci designs flying machines and a parachute. But none of them is ever tested.

1783: French **aviators** (pilots of aircraft) and brothers Joseph and Etienne Montgolfier fly the first hot-air balloon. The brothers heat the air inside the balloon. This causes the air to expand, making it lighter than the air outside the balloon. It floats in the air the way a light object floats in water.

1891: German aviator Otto Lilienthal successfully flies one of the first gliders. A glider's wings catch the air and allow it to soar for a brief time. But the force of gravity soon causes it to land.

1903: US aviators and brothers Orville and Wilbur Wright fly the first aeroplane. The aeroplane is basically a glider with an engine. The engine moves the plane through the air, allowing it to defy gravity as long as the engine has power.

1909: Russian aviator Igor Sikorsky invents the first working helicopter. The whirling blades on a helicopter catch the air like an aeroplane's wings. They produce lift to keep the helicopter in the air.

1947: US pilot Chuck Yeager becomes the first person to fly faster than the speed of sound. That is about 1,225 kilometres (760 miles) per hour.

1957: The Soviet Union (today Russia) launches the first object into space. It is a **satellite** called *Sputnik 1*.

1969: The United States lands astronauts on the moon for the first time.

1981: The US space shuttle *Columbia* becomes the first space shuttle to **orbit** Earth.

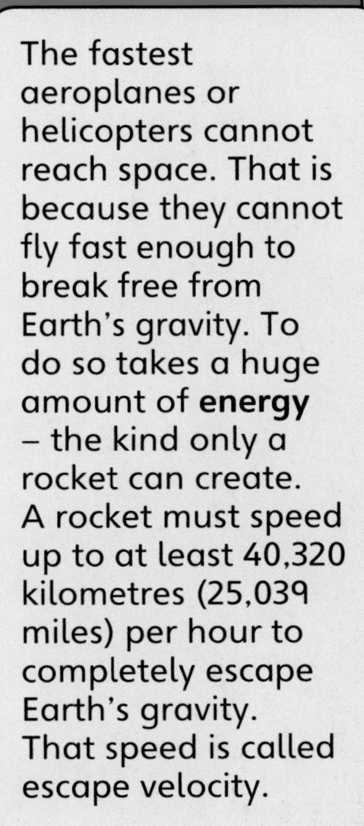

Escaping Earth's gravity

The fastest aeroplanes or helicopters cannot reach space. That is because they cannot fly fast enough to break free from Earth's gravity. To do so takes a huge amount of **energy** – the kind only a rocket can create. A rocket must speed up to at least 40,320 kilometres (25,039 miles) per hour to completely escape Earth's gravity. That speed is called escape velocity.

▼ **This photo shows a trial flight of the Wright brothers' aeroplane.**

Your body and gravity

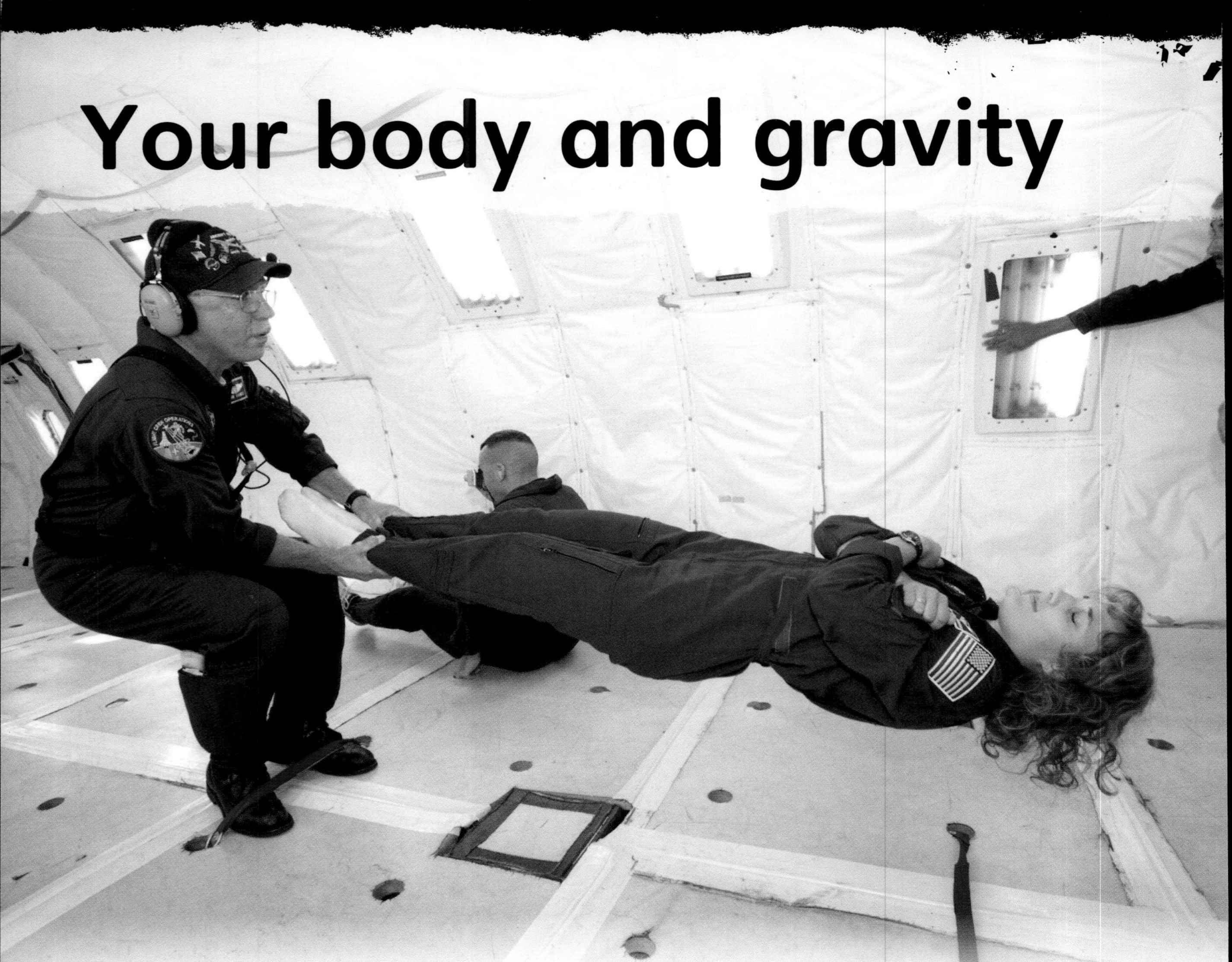

▲ Astronauts train to get used to the lack of gravity in orbit.

Gravity shapes the human body. In fact, it shapes the bodies of all land animals. Bones allow people to stand upright under gravity. Muscles do the same thing. Just getting out of bed is a fight against gravity. Running up a hill or lifting weights is even harder. But we are used to these daily struggles.

Life without gravity

In space there is very little gravity. Astronauts going to the moon float around their spaceships. That looks like fun. But the lack of gravity damages their bodies. Muscles begin to shrink. Some muscles can lose up to 5 per cent of their bulk each week.

Bone loss can be even worse. The bones become thinner. They can break more easily. Even blood is affected. On Earth, gravity pushes the blood in our bodies downwards. But in space, blood floats around more within the body. This causes the body to stop producing as much blood. That in turn weakens the heart. It does not pump as much.

Astronauts have to exercise hard in space. Exercise puts the body under stress the way that gravity does. That helps reduce the problems caused by lack of gravity.

Getting older 

Gravity may be good for us physically. But it does not always help our looks. Human skin becomes less stretchy as people grow older. Gravity pushes down on that sagging skin.

◀ Gravity helps cause wrinkles and bags under the eyes as we grow older.

Find the centre of gravity

Try to balance a pencil on your finger. Move it around until it stays on your finger. The point on the pencil where it balances is its centre of gravity. On a moving person, the centre of gravity shifts around constantly.

The centre of gravity

Pretend you can travel anywhere on magic bathroom scales. At home, the scales show your normal weight. But on Jupiter, they show that you are 318 times your earthly weight. That is because Jupiter is much larger than Earth. Jupiter has a much stronger gravitational pull. Meanwhile, on the moon, your weight drops to one-sixth of your normal weight. The moon is smaller than Earth, so its gravity is much weaker.

Your weight might change. But your **mass** does not. Mass is the amount of **matter** (anything that occupies space) that makes up your body. Regardless of what shape it takes, mass behaves the same way under gravity. The greater the mass, the greater the pull of gravity. All the matter in an object – such as a person – focuses on a single point. That point is called the **centre of gravity**.

▶ To stay on a balance beam, a person must carefully move arms and hips to keep the body's centre of gravity focused on the beam.

High and low centres of gravity

Most sports utility vehicles (SUVs) are taller than cars. That gives them a higher centre of gravity. This means that an SUV is more likely to tip over when turning at high speeds. Knowing the centre of gravity can help people predict how an object moves. People must adjust the way they drive an SUV based on this knowledge.

▼ **The centre of gravity of an SUV is higher than that of most other cars.**

Gravity in space

▲ **Astronauts play with yo-yos and do other activities when training to get used to the low level of gravity on the ISS.**

The International Space Station (ISS) **orbits** Earth. Many people think that there is no **gravity** on the station. They call conditions there "zero-G", meaning "zero gravity". Actually, there is gravity on the station. In fact, Earth's gravity keeps the station in orbit. Scientists call the gravity on the ISS **microgravity**. *Micro* means "really small".

Roller coaster

What is gravity like on the ISS? If you have been on a roller coaster, you have some idea. When the roller coaster reaches the top of a hill at high speed, the people riding it feel weightless for a brief time. That is what it feels like on the ISS all the time. In fact, astronauts train in a special aeroplane called the "Vomit Comet". It makes a series of quick climbs, just like a roller coaster.

To stay in orbit, the station must orbit Earth very fast. It travels at about 28,200 kilometres (17,500 miles) per hour. If Earth had no gravity, the ISS would shoot straight into space. But at 28,200 kilometres per hour, its tendency to fly off is equal to Earth's pull. So, the ISS "falls", or orbits, around Earth. Inside the space station, the crew feels this as near weightlessness, or microgravity.

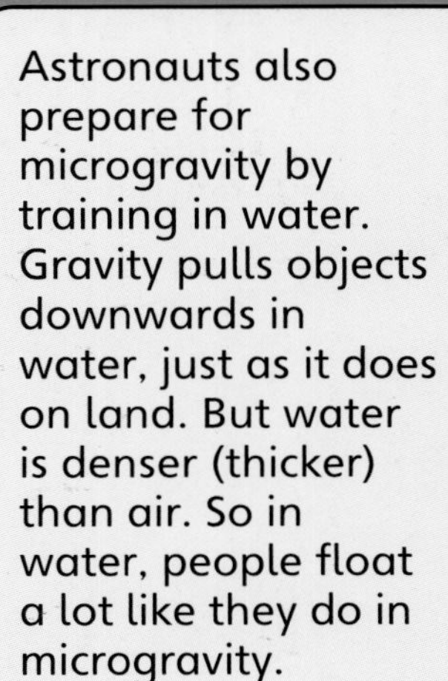

Water treatment

Astronauts also prepare for microgravity by training in water. Gravity pulls objects downwards in water, just as it does on land. But water is denser (thicker) than air. So in water, people float a lot like they do in microgravity.

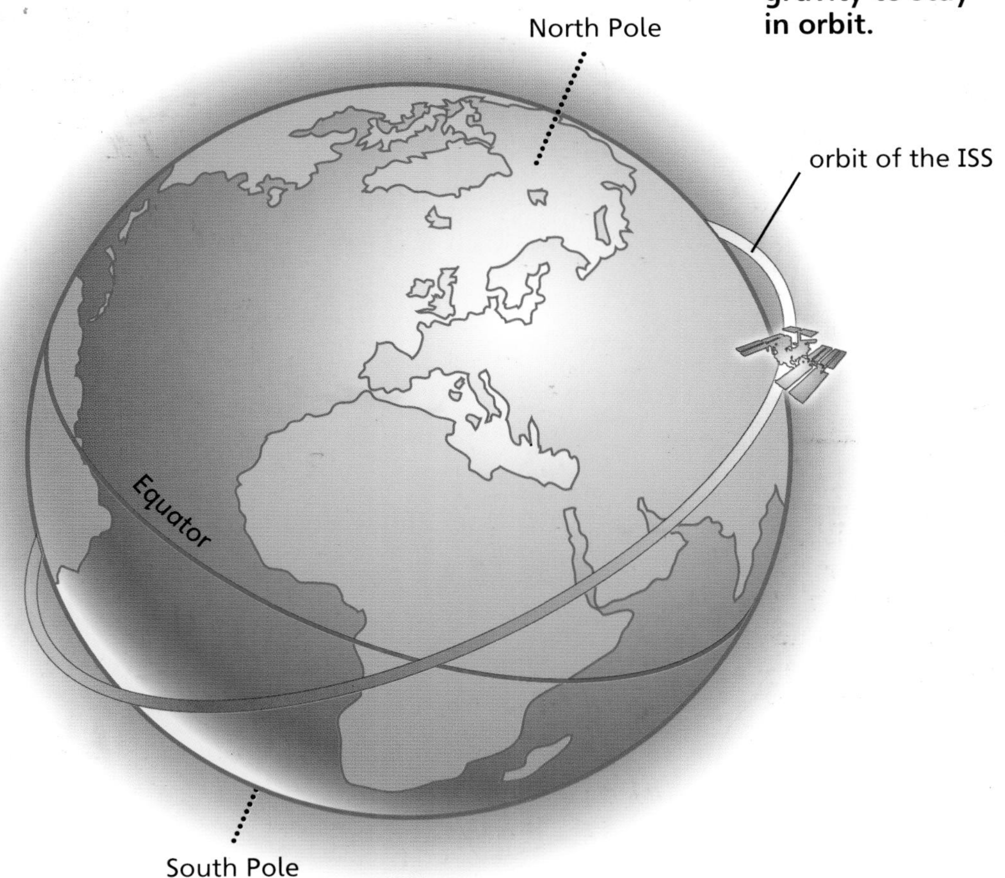

▼ **The ISS needs to balance speed against Earth's gravity to stay in orbit.**

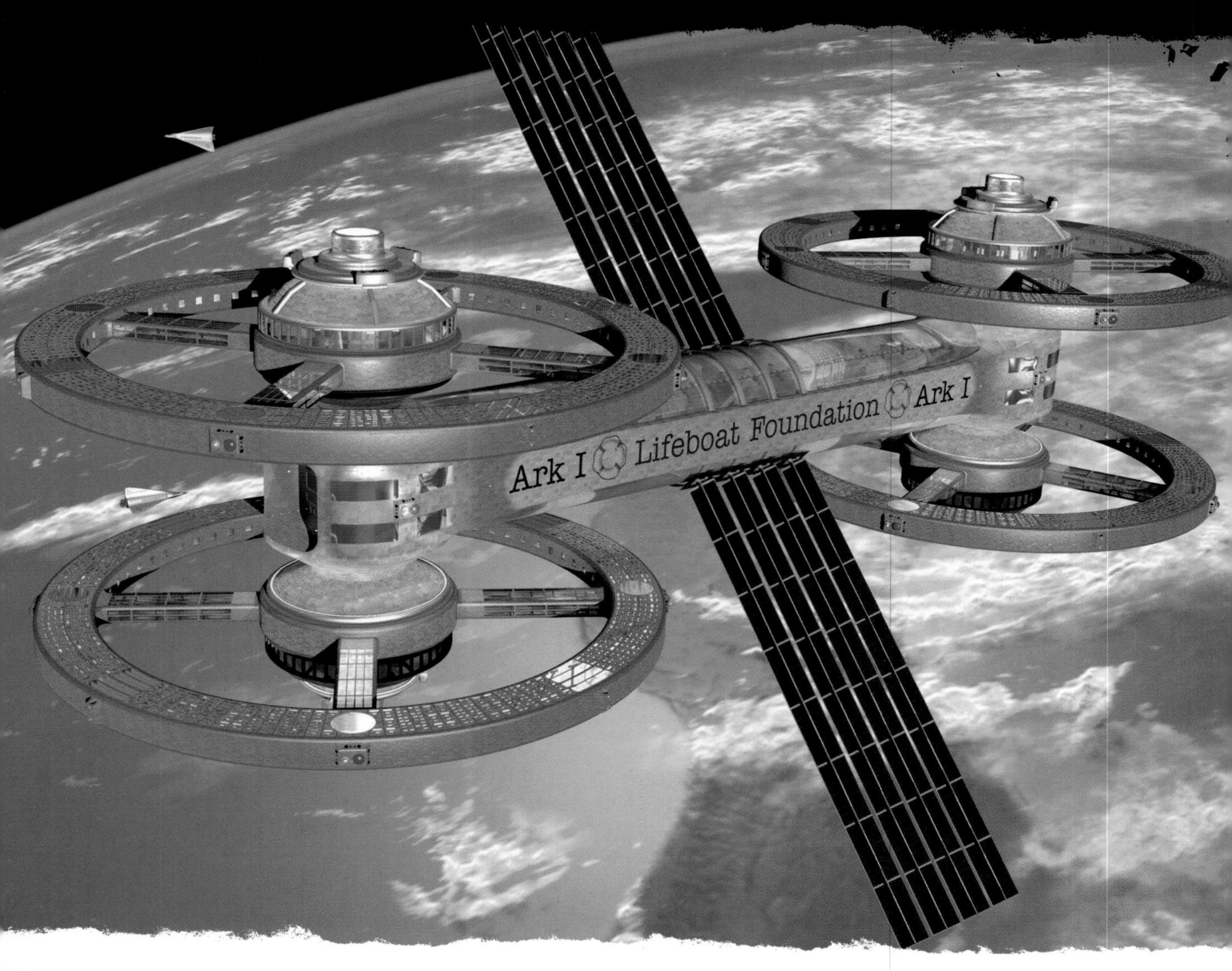

▲ **This is an artist's idea of what a spaceship with artifical gravity might look like.**

Artificial gravity

Humans dream of exploring space. But the lack of gravity there makes space a hard place to live. Bones thin out. The heart and other muscles weaken (see pages 16–17). A journey to a planet close to us, such as Mars, will take several years. Living in low gravity for that long will harm – or maybe even kill – the astronauts.

Scientists have looked for ways to create "artificial gravity". The best way is to make the spaceship into a big centrifuge. A centrifuge is a machine that spins around at a high speed. Think about spinning a bucket of water over your head. If you spin it fast enough, none of the water spills out. The spinning presses the water against the bottom of the bucket.

A spinning spaceship would press people to the sides of the ship. But the spinning would be equal to the force of gravity. So, people would be able to walk around.

Games in microgravity

Despite its dangers, astronauts enjoy life in microgravity. They often make up games to pass the time. Astronauts have come up with weightless basketball and Frisbee™ tosses on space stations. They have also played with footballs while clowning around. Throwing a ball in microgravity can be tricky. On Earth, you have to throw a ball a little high so that gravity brings it back down. But in space, balls and Frisbees™ have to go in straight lines until something makes them stop.

◀ Astronauts do tests to see how the human body adapts to microgravity.

Black holes and wormholes

▲ **This artwork shows the dying sun expanding before intense gravity causes it to collapse into a white dwarf.**

Gravity played a big role in forming Earth. It will play an equally large role in our planet's death. About 5 billion years from now, our sun will run out of fuel. When that happens, the sun will expand to the point where Venus **orbits** today. Then intense gravity will cause it to collapse into a star the size of Earth called a white dwarf. All of this will destroy Earth.

There are many stars much bigger than the sun. When they die out, their deaths will be even more spectacular. Thanks to Einstein's theories, scientists realised that many will result in **black holes**. A black hole is a place in outer space where gravity is so strong that nothing can escape, not even light. Black holes can bend and change both space and time. Humans could not survive entering a black hole. The gravity would crush them.

Shortcut to the stars

Some scientists hope that we will one day find a special type of black hole, called a wormhole. Wormholes are like passageways through space. They are possible in theory. However, none has ever been found. Many people doubt that they exist. But wormholes often appear in films and television programmes. They are used whenever people need a shortcut through space.

How do we know that they are there?

Light cannot escape from black holes. This means we cannot see them. But scientists know black holes exist. This is because we can see their effects. We can see **matter** being pulled into the black hole. We can also see them bend light from nearby stars.

▼ **A black hole is formed when a massive star collapses.**

Gravity's ups and downs

End of the dinosaurs

About 65 million years ago, a very large asteroid hit Earth. It was nearly 10 kilometres (6 miles) wide. It hit what is now southern Mexico. The explosion was huge. Scientists believe that the dust created by it caused the dinosaurs to become **extinct** (die out).

▲ **This artwork shows how a massive asteroid being pulled towards Earth would look.**

Imagine a world in which you could magically switch off **gravity**. Almost everything – including you and this book – would drift off into space.

So, gravity makes life on Earth possible. But it also creates a great danger on our planet. In 1908 a giant space rock called an **asteroid** travelled near our planet. Earth's gravity pulled the asteroid towards Earth. It plunged downwards towards a place called Tunguska in Russia. This house-sized rock exploded with the force of an **atomic bomb**. It could have destroyed a city. Luckily, few people lived near Tunguska.

The 1908 impact was not the first of its kind. Smaller asteroids fall to Earth all the time. When they do, we call them shooting stars or meteors. Most of them burn up in the air before they hit Earth.

Scientists have begun tracking large space rocks that come near Earth. They want to give us warning if something big approaches in the future.

The gravity vacuum cleaner

Our best defence against future asteroid strikes is the gravity of bigger planets. Jupiter has been called the **solar system's** vacuum cleaner. It is so big that its gravity tends to draw large objects away from Earth. In 1994 a **comet** smashed into Jupiter. A comet is a small object in space that orbits the sun. If the comet had hit Earth, it could have killed millions.

▼ **This is an artist's idea of how the 1994 comet would have looked as it headed towards Jupiter.**

Timeline

(These dates are often approximations.)

4.6 billion years ago

Gravity causes ice, dust, and rocks in space to gradually form into our **solar system**.

1490s

Italian artist and inventor Leonardo da Vinci designs some of the first known flying machines. However, he never builds any of them.

1500 CE

early 1600s

Italian scientist Galileo Galilei does gravity experiments. They prove Aristotle wrong. Among other things, Galileo finds that objects of different weights fall at the same speed.

1600

1783

French **aviators** Joseph and Etienne Montgolfier launch the first successful balloon flight.

1800

1891

German aviator Otto Lilienthal successfully flies one of the first gliders.

1900

1903

US aviators Orville and Wilbur Wright fly the first aeroplane.

1905

German-born US scientist Albert Einstein comes up with his General Theory of Relativity. It improves on Newton's ideas about gravity.

1940

1945

The **atomic bomb** is created. Scientists use Einstein's discoveries to create it.

1947

US pilot Chuck Yeager becomes the first person to fly faster than the speed of sound.

1950

1957

The Soviet Union (today Russia) launches the first object into space. It is a **satellite** called *Sputnik 1*.

1960

1969

The United States lands astronauts on the moon for the first time.

1970

This symbol shows where there is a change of scale in the timeline, or where a long period of time with no noted events has been left out.

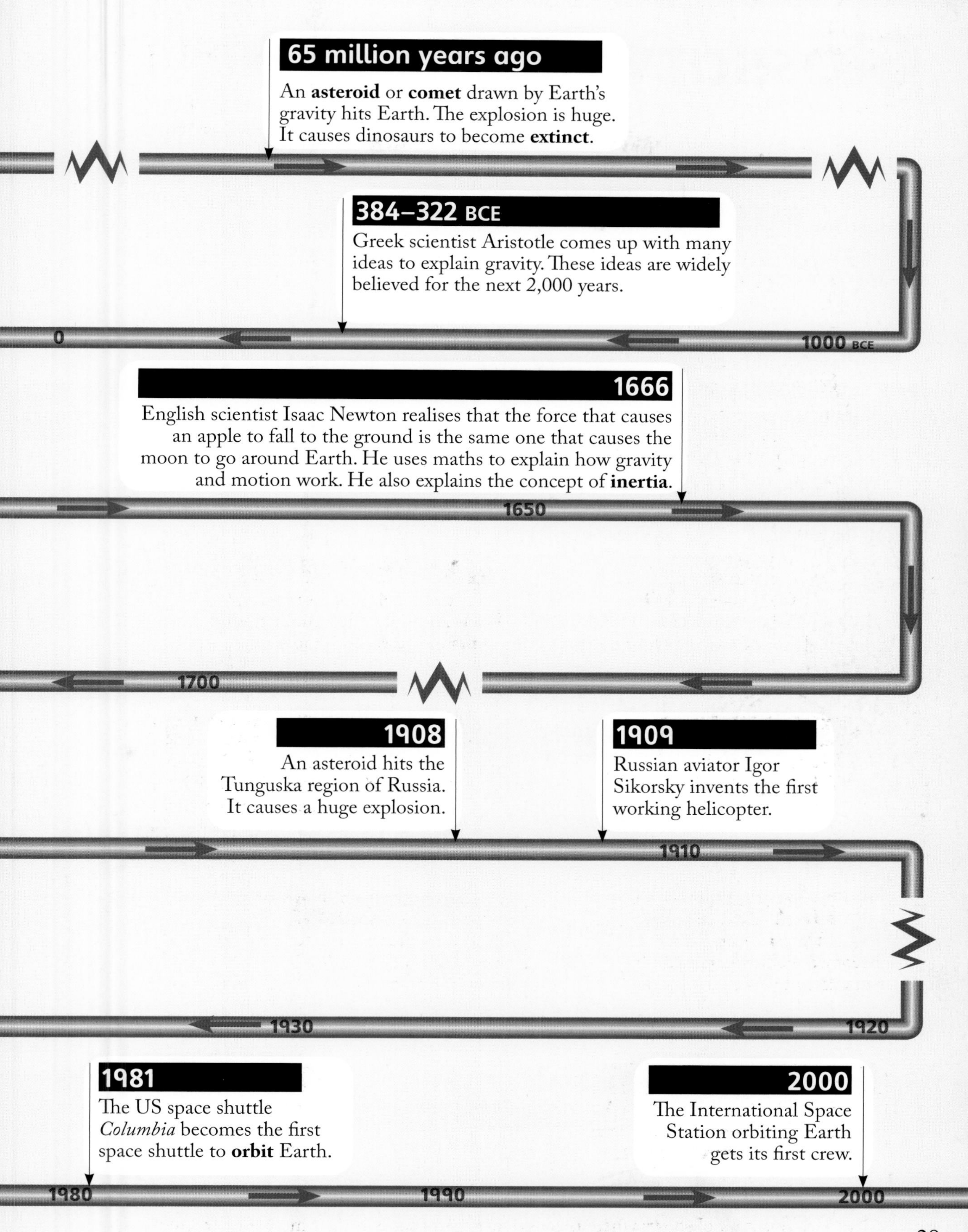
65 million years ago
An **asteroid** or **comet** drawn by Earth's gravity hits Earth. The explosion is huge. It causes dinosaurs to become **extinct**.
384–322 BCE
Greek scientist Aristotle comes up with many ideas to explain gravity. These ideas are widely believed for the next 2,000 years.
0
1000 BCE
1666
English scientist Isaac Newton realises that the force that causes an apple to fall to the ground is the same one that causes the moon to go around Earth. He uses maths to explain how gravity and motion work. He also explains the concept of **inertia**.
1650
1700
1908
An asteroid hits the Tunguska region of Russia. It causes a huge explosion.
1909
Russian aviator Igor Sikorsky invents the first working helicopter.
1910
1930
1920
1981
The US space shuttle *Columbia* becomes the first space shuttle to **orbit** Earth.
2000
The International Space Station orbiting Earth gets its first crew.
1980
1990
2000

Glossary

asteroid type of space rock that orbits the sun. Sometimes Earth's gravity causes asteroids to crash into Earth.

atomic bomb first bomb powerful enough to destroy an entire city. Einstein's equation $E = mc^2$ was used to make the atomic bomb.

aviator pilot of an aircraft. Aviators fly aeroplanes and helicopters.

BCE meaning "before the common era". When this appears after a date, it refers to the time before the Christian religion began. BCE dates are always counted backwards.

black hole place in space where gravity is very strong. Not even light can escape the gravity of a black hole.

CE meaning "common era". When this appears after a date, it refers to the time after the Christian religion began.

centre of gravity focus of gravity in an object. Tightrope walkers must move their arms and legs to keep their centre of gravity on the wire.

comet small object in space that orbits the sun. Comets are usually surrounded by dust and gas, which make them appear to have a tail.

energy a form of power. It takes a great deal of energy to overcome the pull of gravity.

extinct no longer existing. The dinosaurs are extinct.

gravity force of attraction between all objects in the universe. The larger the object is, the greater the pull of its gravity.

inertia an object's resistance to change. Large objects possess more inertia than small objects.

mass size or bulk of an object. Objects with more mass have a stronger gravitational pull.

matter anything that occupies space. All physical objects are made up of matter.

microgravity small amount of gravity. Astronauts on a space shuttle live in microgravity.

orbit curved path around an object. Earth orbits the sun.

satellite object that goes around another object. The moon is a satellite of Earth.

solar system sun and the objects that go around it, including the planets. Our solar system has eight planets.

squared when a number is multiplied by itself. Two squared is four.

universe everything that exists. The universe is made of matter and energy.

Find out more

Books

10 Experiments Your Teacher Never Told You About: Gravity, Andrew Solway (Raintree, 2005)

Albert Einstein, Frieda Wishinsky (Dorling Kindersley, 2005)

E.Guides: Space Travel, Ian Graham (Dorling Kindersley, 2004)

Gravity, Chris Oxlade (Heinemann Library, 2006)

Isaac Newton, Philip Steele (QED Publishing, 2007)

Websites

Visit this website to find some gravity-related science experiments.
http://home.howstuffworks.com/science-projects-for-kids-laws-of-gravity-and-motion.htm

This National Aeronautics and Space Administration (NASA) website helps explain the fundamental laws of the universe, including gravity.
http://spaceplace.nasa.gov/en/kids/cs_universe_laws.shtml

This web page gives a biography of Sir Isaac Newton.
http://www.bbc.co.uk/history/historic_figures/newton_isaac.shtml

Place to visit

Science Museum
Exhibition Road
South Kensington
London SW7 2DD

See the film *Space Station 3D* which shows the effect of reduced gravity on the people working on the International Space Station.

Index